FAVORITE BRAND NAME™

Cooking With Beer

Publications International, Ltd.

Favorite Brand Name Recipes at www.fbnr.com

Microwave Cooking: Microwave ovens vary in wattage. Use the cooking times as guidelines and check for doneness before adding more time.

Preparation/Cooking Times: Preparation times are based on the approximate amount of time required to assemble the recipe before cooking, baking, chilling or serving. These times include preparation steps such as measuring, chopping and mixing. The fact that some preparations and cooking can be done simultaneously is taken into account. Preparation of optional ingredients and serving suggestions is not included.

CONTENTS

Cooking With Beer   6

Soup With a Splash   8
Infuse beer's richness into soups and stews

Draft Picks   24
Perfect food for the big game

Worth the Wait   44
If you spend the time, you'll be glad you did

Beer and Cheese   54
Match the robust flavors of cheese with malt

Hops to It!   66
Just a dash of beer for easy dinners

Sides With Suds   80
Fresh vegetables and side dishes made malty

Acknowledgments   92

Index   93

COOKING with BEER

Enjoy the flavors of malt and hops in food by cooking with beer. Most home cooks use this familiar beverage as an ingredient in casual dishes such as chili or nachos. Beer can also be the base for delicious soups, stews, bastes, marinades, glazes and more.

Beer is actually the generic term for malt beverages typically brewed with barley malt, yeast, hops and water. However, craft breweries and brewpubs across America experiment with other brewing techniques, flavors and ingredients to create different beer styles.

Brewing ingredients vary widely, from classic barley malts made from sprouted, roasted grains of barley; to wheat used in weissbiers; dark roasted chocolate malt used in stouts and porters; fruits such as apricots, cherries and peaches used in seasonal summer brews; and other inventive combinations.

The sugars extracted from barley malts and other grains, honey, and fruits add body and taste. The hops contribute bitterness, ranging from a mild citrus taste to an intense, mouth-puckering bitterness. A well-made beer will balance these flavors.

There are two basic styles of beer. One is top-fermented **ales**, which ferment at warmer temperatures and for a shorter time. Ales often taste somewhat fruitier and are typically more aromatic than lagers.

Lagers are made at colder temperatures, traditionally age for a longer time, and use a different kind of bottom-fermenting yeast. Lagers may taste crisper and drier when compared to ales; often, the carbonation is greater, too.

The following charts list the most widely distributed beer styles in North America, along with some of their possible culinary uses.

ALES

India Pale Ale	Often very hoppy. In cooking, use in place of wine or vinegar.
American Amber	Some malt body. Use in place of broth or stock.
Brown Ale	Good caramel notes and mild flavor. Use in marinades.
Porter	Deep brown color and toasty flavor. Use in sauces.
Stout	Dark, black or mahogany; very roasty. Use in gravies and barbecue sauces.

LAGERS

Pilsner	The most popular and best known style in North America. Used widely in cooking and baking, especially in biscuits, fritters and batters for seafood.
Bock	Some caramel notes, with a big body. Excellent with beef or pork.
Dark Lager	Milder body than bock, but still very good with roast meats.
Malt Liquor	May be used with sauces and glazes—and it's great with onion rings.

FRUIT BEER

Pêche Lambic (Peach)	Use with chicken or poultry.
Kriek Lambic (Cherry)	Delicious with sauces or desserts.
Framboise Lambic (Raspberry)	Use in glazes for seafood.

BELGIAN ALES

Strong Ale	Wonderful with cheeses and dips.
Witbier	A delicate base for poached seafood or fritters.
Dubbel or Tripel	Use in carbonnade, soups and stews.

SOUP
with a
SPLASH

Infuse Beer's Richness into Soups and Stews

Hearty Beefy Beer Soup

1 tablespoon vegetable oil
$^3/_4$ pound round steak, cut into $^1/_2$-inch cubes
1 large onion, chopped
2 medium carrots, sliced
2 ribs celery, diced
5 cups Beef Stock (recipe follows) or canned beef broth
1 bottle (12 ounces) stout or dark ale
$^3/_4$ teaspoon dried oregano leaves, crushed
$^1/_4$ teaspoon salt
$^1/_8$ teaspoon black pepper
1 small zucchini, cut into $^1/_2$-inch cubes
4 ounces mushrooms, sliced
1 can (15 ounces) kidney beans, drained
Fresh herb sprig for garnish

1. Heat oil in 5-quart Dutch oven over medium heat. Add beef, onion, carrots and celery to hot oil. Cook and stir until meat is no longer pink and carrots and celery are slightly tender. Remove from heat.

continued on page 10

Hearty Beefy Beer Soup

Hearty Beefy Beer Soup, continued

2. Stir in Beef Stock, stout, oregano, salt and pepper. Bring to a boil over high heat. Reduce heat to medium-low; simmer, uncovered, 45 minutes.

3. Stir zucchini, mushrooms and kidney beans into soup. Bring to a boil over high heat. Reduce heat to medium-low; simmer, uncovered, about 5 minutes or until zucchini is tender. Ladle into bowls. Garnish, if desired. *Makes 6 servings*

Beef Stock

    4 pounds meaty beef bones
    2 large onions
    2 large carrots, halved
    4 ribs celery, halved
3½ quarts (14 cups) cold water, divided
    8 sprigs parsley
    2 bay leaves
    1 teaspoon dried thyme leaves, crushed
    6 black peppercorns
    3 whole cloves

1. Preheat oven to 450°F. Rinse bones in cold water; arrange in large roasting pan. Brown bones in oven 30 minutes, turning once during cooking.

2. Trim tops and roots from onions, leaving most of the dried outer skin intact; cut into wedges.

3. Arrange onions, carrots and celery over bones. Roast 30 minutes more.*

4. Remove bones and vegetables from roasting pan and place in stockpot or 5-quart Dutch oven. Skim fat from roasting pan.

5. To deglaze pan, pour 2 cups water into pan. Place over burners and cook over medium-high heat, scraping up brown bits and stirring constantly 2 to 3 minutes or until mixture is reduced by about half. Transfer mixture to stockpot.

6. Add remaining 3 quarts (12 cups) water, parsley, bay leaves, thyme, peppercorns and cloves to stockpot. Bring to a boil over high heat. Reduce heat to medium-low; simmer, uncovered, 3 to 4 hours. Skim foam that rises to the top.

7. Remove stock from heat and cool slightly. Remove large bones. Strain stock through large sieve or colander lined with several layers of damp cheesecloth; remove and discard bones and vegetables.

8. Use immediately, refrigerate in tightly covered container up to 2 days, or freeze in storage containers for several months.

Makes about 1½ quarts stock

*For added zip, spread 3 ounces tomato paste over bones at this point. Roast an additional 15 minutes. Proceed as directed in step 4.

Wisconsin Cheddar, Swiss and Beer Soup

    2 cups onion, diced
    2 tablespoons garlic, chopped
    1 cup butter
 ½ cup flour
    2 quarts milk
    2 bay leaves
    3 cups (12 ounces) Wisconsin medium Cheddar, shredded
    3 cups (12 ounces) Wisconsin aged Swiss, shredded
       Salt and pepper to taste
    1 pinch nutmeg
1½ cups pale ale

Sauté onion and garlic in butter until soft, about 5 minutes. Add flour; cook, stirring frequently over medium heat, about 5 minutes. Whisk in milk. Add bay leaves; cook, stirring constantly over low heat until mixture thickens, about 20 minutes. Stir in cheeses gradually; cook just until cheese melts. Remove from heat. Season with salt, pepper and nutmeg; remove bay leaves. Stir in pale ale and serve.

Makes 8 servings

Favorite recipe from **Wisconsin Milk Marketing Board**

Farmer's Market Grilled Chowder

1 ear fresh corn *or* 1 cup frozen corn, thawed
1 small zucchini, cut lengthwise into $^1/_4$-inch-thick slices
   Nonstick cooking spray
1 large potato
1 tablespoon margarine
$^1/_2$ cup chopped onion
2 tablespoons all-purpose flour
$^1/_2$ teaspoon salt
$^1/_2$ teaspoon dried thyme leaves
$^1/_8$ teaspoon white pepper
1 cup wheat beer (weissbier)
1 cup lowfat (1%) milk
$^1/_2$ cup (2 ounces) shredded reduced-fat sharp Cheddar cheese

1. Remove husks and silk from corn. Place in large bowl and cover with cold water; soak 20 to 30 minutes. Remove; wrap in foil. Grill on covered grill over medium-hot coals 20 to 25 minutes or until hot and tender, turning over halfway through grilling time. Remove kernels from cob. Set aside.

2. To grill zucchini, spray zucchini on both sides with cooking spray. Grill on uncovered grill over medium coals 4 minutes or until grillmarked and tender, turning once during grilling. Cool; cut into bite-size pieces. Set aside.

3. Cut potato in half lengthwise; grill potato halves on covered grill over medium coals 15 to 20 minutes or until potato is tender, turning over once during grilling. Cut potato into cubes.

4. Melt margarine in large saucepan over medium heat. Add onion; cook and stir 5 minutes or until tender but not brown. Stir in flour, salt, thyme and pepper. Cook and stir about 1 minute.

5. Stir beer and milk into flour mixture. Cook and stir over medium heat until mixture begins to bubble; continue cooking about 1 minute more. Stir in corn, zucchini, potato and cheese. Reduce heat to low; simmer, uncovered, until cheese is melted and mixture is hot, stirring constantly. Garnish as desired.   *Makes 4 servings*

Farmer's Market Grilled Chowder

Durango Chili

3 tablespoons vegetable oil, divided
1 pound 95% lean ground beef
1 pound boneless beef top sirloin steak, cut into $^1/_2$-inch cubes
2 medium onions, chopped
1 green bell pepper, seeded and chopped
4 cloves garlic, minced
$^1/_4$ cup tomato paste
3 to 5 fresh or canned jalapeño peppers,* stemmed, seeded
    and minced
2 bay leaves
5 tablespoons chili powder
1 teaspoon salt
1 teaspoon ground cumin
$^1/_2$ teaspoon black pepper
2 cans (14$^1/_2$ ounces each) whole tomatoes, undrained
1 bottle (12 ounces) dark lager or bock beer
1 can (10$^3/_4$ ounces) condensed beef broth *plus* 1 can water
2 cans (4 ounces each) diced green chilies, undrained
3 cups cooked pinto beans *or* 2 cans (15 ounces each) pinto or
    kidney beans, drained

Condiments
    1 cup (4 ounces) shredded Cheddar cheese
    $^1/_2$ cup sour cream
    4 green onions with tops, thinly sliced
    1 can (2$^1/_4$ ounces) sliced pitted ripe olives, drained

Jalapeño peppers can sting and irritate the skin; wear rubber gloves when handling peppers and do not touch eyes. Wash hands after handling peppers.

Heat 1 tablespoon oil in 5-quart Dutch oven over medium-high heat. Add ground beef, stirring to separate meat; add cubed beef. Cook, stirring occasionally, until meat is lightly browned. Transfer meat and pan drippings to medium bowl. Heat remaining 2 tablespoons oil in

continued on page 16

Durango Chili

Durango Chili, continued

Dutch oven over medium heat. Add onions, bell pepper and garlic. Cook until vegetables are tender. Stir in tomato paste, jalapeño peppers, bay leaves, chili powder, salt, cumin and black pepper. Coarsely chop tomatoes; add to Dutch oven. Add meat, beer, broth, water and green chilies; bring to a boil. Reduce heat and simmer, partially covered, 2 hours or until meat is very tender and chili has thickened slightly. Stir in beans. Simmer, uncovered, 20 minutes. For thicker chili, continue simmering, uncovered, until chili is of desired consistency. Remove and discard bay leaves. Spoon into individual bowls. Serve with condiments. *Makes 6 servings*

Kielbasa & Cabbage Soup

1 pound Polish kielbasa, cut into $1/2$-inch cubes
1 package (16 ounces) coleslaw mix (shredded green cabbage and carrots)
3 cans ($14^1/2$ ounces each) beef broth
1 can (12 ounces) beer or nonalcoholic malt beverage
1 cup water
$1/2$ teaspoon caraway seeds
2 cups *French's*® French Fried Onions, divided
Garnish: fresh dill sprigs (optional)

1. Coat 5-quart pot or Dutch oven with nonstick cooking spray. Cook kielbasa over medium-high heat about 5 minutes or until browned. Add coleslaw mix; sauté until tender.

2. Add broth, beer, water, caraway seeds and *1 cup* French Fried Onions; bring to a boil over medium-high heat. Reduce heat to low. Simmer, uncovered, 10 minutes to blend flavors. Spoon soup into serving bowls; top with remaining onions. Garnish with fresh dill sprigs, if desired. *Makes 8 servings*

Prep Time: 10 minutes
Cook Time: 20 minutes

Ham and Beer Cheese Soup

    1 cup chopped onion
$^1/_2$ cup sliced celery
    2 tablespoons butter or margarine
    1 cup hot water
    1 HERB-OX® chicken flavor bouillon cube *or* 1 teaspoon
        instant chicken boullion
    3 cups half-and-half
    3 cups (18 ounces) diced CURE 81® ham
    1 (16-ounce) loaf pasteurized process cheese spread, cubed
    1 (12-ounce) can beer
    3 tablespoons all-purpose flour
        Popcorn (optional)

In Dutch oven over medium-high heat, sauté onion and celery in butter until tender. In small liquid measuring cup, combine water and bouillon; set aside. Add half-and-half, ham, cheese, beer and $^3/_4$ cup broth to onion and celery mixture. Cook, stirring constantly, until cheese melts. Combine remaining $^1/_4$ cup broth and flour; stir until smooth. Add flour mixture to soup, stirring constantly. Cook, stirring constantly, until slightly thickened. Sprinkle individual servings with popcorn, if desired.   *Makes 8 servings*

Tip: Use a mild pilsner lager for smooth flavor.

Deviled Beef Short Rib Stew

4 pounds beef short ribs, trimmed
2 pounds small red potatoes, scrubbed and scored
8 carrots, peeled and cut into chunks
2 onions, cut into thick wedges
1 bottle (12 ounces) beer or non-alcoholic malt beverage
8 tablespoons *French's*® Bold n' Spicy Brown Mustard, divided
3 tablespoons *French's*® Worcestershire Sauce, divided
2 tablespoons cornstarch

Slow Cooker Directions

1. Broil ribs 6 inches from heat on rack in broiler pan 10 minutes or until well browned, turning once. Place vegetables in bottom of slow cooker. Place ribs on top of vegetables.

2. Combine beer, *6 tablespoons* mustard and *2 tablespoons* Worcestershire in medium bowl. Pour into slow cooker. Cover and cook on high 5 hours* or until meat is tender.

3. Transfer meat and vegetables to platter; keep warm. Strain fat from broth; pour broth into saucepan. Combine cornstarch with *2 tablespoons cold water* in small bowl. Stir into broth with remaining *2 tablespoons* mustard and *1 tablespoon* Worcestershire. Heat to boiling. Reduce heat to medium-low. Cook 1 to 2 minutes or until thickened, stirring often. Pass gravy with meat and vegetables. Serve meat with additional mustard.   *Makes 6 servings (with 3 cups gravy)*

Or cook 10 hours on low.

Hint: Prepare ingredients the night before for quick assembly in the morning. Keep refrigerated until ready to use.

Tip: Use a barleywine or spiced winter ale in this stew for an even bolder beef flavor.

Deviled Beef Short Rib Stew

Wisconsin Sausage Soup

1/2 cup butter
1 onion, chopped
1 carrot, chopped
1 teaspoon minced garlic
1 cup all-purpose flour
2 cups chicken broth
2 cups milk
3/4 cup beer
1 teaspoon Worcestershire sauce
1/2 teaspoon salt
1/2 teaspoon dry mustard
1 bay leaf
7 ounces Cheddar cheese, shredded
3 ounces Swiss cheese, shredded
1/2 pound HILLSHIRE FARM® Smoked Sausage

Melt butter in medium saucepan over medium heat. Add onion, carrot and garlic; sauté until softened. Add flour; cook 5 minutes, stirring often. Add chicken broth, milk, beer, Worcestershire sauce, salt, mustard and bay leaf. Reduce heat to low; cook until soup has thickened, whisking often. Remove and discard bay leaf.

Slowly whisk cheeses into soup until combined and smooth. Cut Smoked Sausage lengthwise into quarters, then slice into 1/2-inch pieces. Sauté sausage in small skillet over medium-high heat until heated through. Blot excess grease with paper towels; add sausage to soup. Serve soup hot. *Makes 8 to 10 servings*

Tip: Use a bock beer to enhance the savory sausage flavor of this soup.

Mussels in Beer Broth Over Pasta

2 pounds mussels, scrubbed and soaked
8 ounces uncooked fettuccine pasta
2 tablespoons olive oil
1 bottle (12 ounces) Belgian brown ale
2 shallots, chopped *or* ⅓ cup chopped onion
1 clove garlic, minced
¼ teaspoon fennel seeds, crushed
1 bulb fresh fennel, peeled and cubed
1 cup coarsely chopped fresh plum tomatoes
2 tablespoons chopped fresh parsley and grated fresh
    Parmesan cheese, for garnish

1. Discard any mussels that remain open when tapped with fingers.

2. Cook fettuccine according to package directions; drain. Place fettuccine in large bowl; toss with oil. Cover to keep warm.

3. Meanwhile, combine ale, shallots, garlic and fennel seeds in large stockpot. Bring to a boil over high heat. Cover and boil 3 minutes. Add mussels. Cover; reduce heat to medium. Steam 5 to 7 minutes or until mussels are opened. Remove from stockpot with slotted spoon; set aside. Discard any unopened mussels.

4. Simmer, uncovered, until liquid is reduced to about 1 cup. Add cubed fennel; simmer 1 to 2 minutes. Add tomatoes; remove from heat.

5. Divide fettuccine between 4 pasta bowls. Spoon mussels over noodles and pour sauce on top. Garnish, if desired. Serve immediately.   *Makes 4 servings*

Mussels in Beer Broth Over Pasta

DRAFT PICKS

Perfect Food for the Big Game

Brats in Beer

1½ pounds bratwurst links (about 5 or 6)
1 bottle (12 ounces) amber ale
1 medium onion, thinly sliced
2 tablespoons brown sugar
2 tablespoons red wine or cider vinegar
Mustard
Cocktail rye bread

Slow Cooker Directions

1. Place bratwurst, amber ale, onion, brown sugar and vinegar in slow cooker. Cover; cook on LOW 4 to 5 hours.

2. Remove bratwurst from cooking liquid. Cut into ½-inch-thick slices. For mini open-faced sandwiches, spread mustard on cocktail rye bread. Top with bratwurst slices and onion, if desired. Arrange on platter.

Makes 5 to 6 servings

Prep Time: 5 minutes
Cook Time: 4 to 5 hours

Brats in Beer

Borracho Beef

1 bottle (12 ounces) dark beer
¼ cup reduced-sodium soy sauce
3 cloves garlic, minced
1 teaspoon ground cumin
1 teaspoon ground chili powder
½ teaspoon ground red pepper
1 beef flank steak (about 1 pound)
6 medium red, yellow or green bell peppers, seeded and cut
    lengthwise into quarters
8 (6- to 8-inch) flour tortillas
  Sour cream
  Salsa

1. Combine beer, soy sauce, garlic, cumin, chili powder and red pepper in large resealable plastic food storage bag; knead bag to combine. Add beef and seal. Refrigerate up to 24 hours, turning occasionally.

2. Preheat grill. Remove beef from marinade; discard remaining marinade. Place steak on grid over medium heat. Grill, uncovered, 17 to 21 minutes for medium rare to medium or until desired doneness, turning once during grilling. Grill bell peppers 7 to 10 minutes or until tender, turning once.

3. Cut steak across the grain into thin slices and serve with bell peppers, tortillas, sour cream and salsa. *Makes 4 servings*

Make-Ahead Time: up to 1 day before serving
Final Prep Time: 20 minutes

Borracho Beef

Spicy Ale Shrimp

3 bottles (12 ounces each) pilsner beer, divided
1 tablespoon seafood boil seasoning blend
1 teaspoon mustard seeds
1 teaspoon red pepper flakes
1 lemon, sliced into quarters
1 pound raw large shrimp (15 to 20 count), deveined and
    shelled except for tails
Dipping Sauce (recipe follows)

1. Pour one bottle of beer into large bowl half-filled with ice; set aside.

2. Add remaining 2 bottles of beer, seafood boil seasoning, mustard seeds and red pepper flakes to 1-gallon stockpot. Squeeze lemon juice into pot; add lemon quarters. Bring beer mixture to a simmer over medium-high heat.

3. Add shrimp. Cover; remove from heat. Let sit 3 minutes to cook shrimp. Drain; transfer shrimp to bowl of chilled beer and ice cubes. When cool, remove shrimp from bowl and arrange on platter. Serve with Dipping Sauce. *Makes 15 to 20 shrimp*

Dipping Sauce

1 cup ketchup
1 tablespoon chili-garlic paste
1 tablespoon grated horseradish
    Juice of one lime
    Hot pepper sauce

Combine ketchup, chili-garlic paste, horseradish and lime juice in small glass bowl. Add hot pepper sauce to taste; mix well. Cover and refrigerate 1 hour.

Spicy Ale Shrimp

Cajun Chicken Nuggets & Grilled Fruit

$^1\!/_2$ cup beer or non-alcoholic malt beverage
$^1\!/_4$ cup *French's®* Bold n' Spicy Brown Mustard
  2 tablespoons oil
  1 pound boneless skinless chicken breasts, cut into $1^1\!/_2$-inch
      pieces
$^3\!/_4$ cup plain dry bread crumbs
  1 tablespoon plus 1 teaspoon prepared Cajun seasoning blend
  1 pineapple, peeled, cored and cut into $^1\!/_2$-inch-thick rings
  2 peaches, cut into 1-inch-thick wedges

1. Combine beer, mustard and oil in large bowl. Add chicken pieces; toss to coat evenly. Cover and marinate in refrigerator 20 minutes.

2. Preheat oven to 350°F. Coat baking sheet with nonstick cooking spray. Combine bread crumbs and cajun seasoning in pie plate. Remove chicken from marinade; roll in bread crumb mixture to coat. Discard any remaining marinade. Place chicken on prepared baking sheet. Bake 20 minutes or until lightly golden brown and no longer pink in center, turning once. Remove to serving plate.

3. Coat fruit with nonstick cooking spray. Place fruit on oiled grid. Grill 5 to 8 minutes over medium heat until just tender. Serve with chicken nuggets and Peachy Mustard Glaze (recipe follows).

Makes 4 servings

Prep Time: 20 minutes
Marinate Time: 20 minutes
Cook Time: 20 minutes

Peachy Mustard Glaze

$^3\!/_4$ cup peach preserves
$^1\!/_4$ cup *French's®* Classic Yellow® Mustard
  2 tablespoons orange juice

Microwave preserves in small bowl on HIGH (100%) 2 minutes or until melted, stirring once. Stir in mustard and juice.

Makes 1 cup glaze

Prep Time: 5 minutes

Dark Ale and Dill Burgers

1 pound 95% lean ground beef
¾ cup shredded zucchini
⅓ cup shredded carrots
2 tablespoons finely minced onion
2 tablespoons finely minced garlic (12 cloves)
2 tablespoons chopped fresh dill
1 egg, beaten
½ cup dark ale
1 teaspoon salt
½ teaspoon red pepper flakes
4 whole wheat buns or rye rolls (optional)

1. Preheat grill. Combine ground beef, zucchini, carrots, onion, garlic and dill in large bowl; mix lightly. Combine egg, ale, salt and red pepper flakes in medium bowl. Add to ground beef mixture; mix lightly. Shape into 4 patties.

2. Grill over medium heat, covered, 8 to 10 minutes (or, uncovered, 13 to 15 minutes) to medium (160°F), turning once. Serve on whole wheat buns or rye rolls, if desired. *Makes 4 servings*

Porter Portobello Mushrooms

1 pound lean ground lamb
2 tablespoons drained finely chopped pimiento
2 teaspoons minced garlic (4 cloves)
1 teaspoon *each* chopped chives and chopped fresh rosemary
½ teaspoon red pepper flakes
10 large portobello mushroom caps
1 bottle (12 ounces) porter ale

1. Preheat oven to 350°F. Thoroughly mix ground lamb, pimiento, garlic, chives, rosemary and red pepper flakes in medium bowl.

2. Remove stems from mushrooms; stuff mushroom caps with lamb mixture. Place stuffed mushrooms in 13×9-inch baking pan; pour ale over mushrooms. Bake about 20 minutes or until meat is browned. *Makes 10 servings*

Bock Bean Bites

1 cup chunky salsa
1 cup refried beans
$1/4$ cup bock beer or dark lager
2 tablespoons canned minced chilies
2 tablespoons chopped fresh cilantro
$1/2$ teaspoon ground cumin
3 large (10-inch) flour tortillas
1 cup (4 ounces) shredded Mexican cheese blend

1. Pour salsa into strainer; let drain at least 20 minutes.

2. Meanwhile, combine refried beans, beer, chilies, cilantro and cumin in small bowl; mix well. Preheat oven to 400°F. Spray baking sheet lightly with nonstick cooking spray; set aside.

3. Cut each tortilla into $2^{1}/_{2}$-inch circles, using round cookie cutter (9 to 10 circles per tortilla). Spread each tortilla circle with refried bean mixture, leaving $1/4$ inch around edge. Top each with heaping teaspoonful drained salsa; sprinkle with about 1 teaspoon cheese.

4. Place tortillas on prepared baking sheet. Bake about 7 minutes or until tortillas are golden brown. *Makes about 30 servings*

Bock Bean Bites

Brats 'n' Beer

1 bottle (12 ounces) amber ale
4 bratwurst (about 1 pound)
1 sweet or Spanish onion, thinly sliced and separated into
    rings
1 tablespoon olive oil
$^1\!/_4$ teaspoon salt
$^1\!/_4$ teaspoon black pepper
4 hot dog rolls

1. Prepare coals for direct grilling.

2. Pour amber ale into heavy medium saucepan with ovenproof handle. (If not ovenproof, wrap heavy-duty foil around handle.) Place saucepan on grill.

3. Pierce bratwurst with knife; add to beer. Simmer, uncovered, over medium coals 15 minutes, turning once during cooking.

4. Place onion rings on heavy-duty foil. Drizzle with oil; sprinkle with salt and pepper. Fold sides of foil over rings to enclose. Place onion slices on grill. Grill, uncovered, 10 to 15 minutes or until onion slices are tender.

5. Transfer bratwurst to grill. Remove saucepan from grill; discard beer. Grill bratwurst 10 minutes or until browned and cooked through, turning once during grilling.

6. Place bratwurst in rolls. Top with onions. Garnish as desired.

Makes 4 servings

Stout Beef Bundles

1 pound ground beef
$\frac{1}{2}$ cup sliced green onions
1 medium clove garlic, minced
$\frac{2}{3}$ cup chopped water chestnuts
$\frac{1}{2}$ cup chopped red bell pepper
2 tablespoons hoisin sauce
1 tablespoon soy sauce
$\frac{1}{4}$ cup stout
2 tablespoons chopped fresh cilantro
1 or 2 heads leaf lettuce, separated into leaves (discard outer leaves)

1. Brown ground beef in medium skillet. Drain. Add onions and garlic. Cook until tender. Stir in water chestnuts, bell pepper, hoisin, soy sauce and stout. Cook, stirring occasionally, until bell pepper is crisp-tender and most of liquid has evaporated. Remove from heat.

2. Stir in cilantro. Spoon ground beef mixture onto lettuce leaves; sprinkle with additional hoisin sauce, if desired. Wrap lettuce leaf around ground beef mixture to make appetizer bundle.

Makes 8 appetizer servings

Tip: Slice additional green onions into long strips and use to tie leaves in place around bundles.

Stout Beef Bundles

Chicken Wings in Cerveza

1½ pounds chicken wings or drummettes
1 teaspoon salt
1 teaspoon dried thyme
⅛ teaspoon black pepper
1 bottle (12 ounces) Mexican beer

1. Cut off and discard wing tips. Cut each wing in half at joint. Place chicken in shallow bowl; sprinkle with salt, thyme and pepper. Pour beer over chicken; toss to coat. Cover and refrigerate 2 hours or up to 6 hours.

2. Preheat oven to 375°F. Line shallow baking pan with foil; spray with nonstick cooking spray.

3. Drain chicken, reserving marinade. Arrange chicken on prepared pan in single layer. Bake 40 minutes or until chicken is well browned on all sides, turning and basting with reserved marinade occasionally. *Do not brush with marinade during last 5 minutes of baking.* Discard remaining marinade. Serve warm or at room temperature.

Makes 4 servings

Chicken Wings in Cerveza

Spicy Italian Beef

1 boneless beef chuck roast (3 to 4 pounds)
1 jar (12 ounces) peperoncini
1 can (14$\frac{1}{2}$ ounces) beef broth
1 bottle (12 ounces) amber ale
1 onion, peeled and minced
2 tablespoons Italian herb blend
1 loaf French bread, cut into thick slices
10 slices provolone cheese (optional)

Slow Cooker Directions

1. Trim fat from roast. Cut roast, if necessary, to fit in slow cooker, leaving meat in as many large pieces as possible.

2. Drain peppers; pull off stem ends and discard. Add peppers, broth, ale, onion and herb blend to slow cooker; *do not stir.* Cover; cook on LOW 8 to 10 hours.

3. Remove meat from slow cooker; shred with 2 forks. Return shredded meat to slow cooker; mix well.

4. Serve on French bread, topped with cheese, if desired. Add additional sauce and peppers as desired.   *Makes 8 to 10 servings*

Tip: Peperoncini are thin, 2- to 3-inch-long pickled mild peppers. Look for them in the Italian foods or pickled foods section of the grocery store.

Spicy Italian Beef

WORTH the WAIT

If You Spend the Time, You'll Be Glad You Did

Ale'd Pork and Sauerkraut

32 ounces sauerkraut, undrained
1$\frac{1}{2}$ tablespoons sugar
1 can (12 ounces) dark beer or ale
3$\frac{1}{2}$ pounds pork shoulder or pork butt
$\frac{1}{2}$ teaspoon salt
$\frac{1}{4}$ teaspoon garlic powder
$\frac{1}{4}$ teaspoon black pepper
Paprika

Slow Cooker Directions

1. Pour sauerkraut into slow cooker. Sprinkle sugar evenly over sauerkraut; pour beer over all. Place pork, fat side up, on top of sauerkraut mixture; sprinkle evenly with remaining ingredients. Cover and cook on HIGH 6 hours.

2. Place pork on serving platter. Using slotted spoon, remove sauerkraut and arrange around pork. Spoon about $\frac{1}{2}$ to $\frac{3}{4}$ cup cooking liquid over sauerkraut, if desired. *Makes 6 to 8 servings*

Ale'd Pork and Sauerkraut

Grilled Chicken With Chili Beer Baste

2 tablespoons vegetable oil
1 small onion, chopped
1 clove garlic, minced
$^{1}/_{2}$ cup ketchup
2 tablespoons brown sugar
2 teaspoons chili powder
2 chipotle peppers in adobo sauce, minced
1 teaspoon dry mustard
$^{1}/_{2}$ teaspoon *each* salt and black pepper
3 bottles (12 ounces each) pilsner beer, divided
$^{1}/_{2}$ cup tomato juice
$^{1}/_{4}$ cup Worcestershire sauce
1 tablespoon lemon juice
2 whole chickens (about $3^{1}/_{2}$ pounds each), cut up

1. Make Chili Beer Baste. Heat oil in 2-quart saucepan over medium heat. Add onion and garlic; cook until onion is tender. Combine ketchup, brown sugar, chili powder, chipotles, dry mustard, salt and pepper in medium bowl. Add 1 bottle of beer, tomato juice, Worcestershire sauce and lemon juice; whisk until well blended. Pour mixture into saucepan with onion and garlic. Bring to a simmer; cook until sauce has thickened slightly and is reduced to about 2 cups. Let cool. Refrigerate overnight.

2. Place chicken pieces in 2 large resealable plastic food storage bags. Pour remaining 2 bottles beer over chicken in both bags; seal bags. Refrigerate 8 hours or overnight.

3. Preheat charcoal grill and grease grill rack. Remove chickens from beer marinade; drain well. Discard marinade. Place chicken leg and thigh quarters on hottest part of grill 4 to 6 inches above solid bed of coals (coals should be evenly covered with gray ashes); place breast pieces on cooler edges of grill. Cook, turning occasionally, 25 to 30 minutes.

continued on page 48

Grilled Chicken With Chili Beer Baste

Grilled Chicken With Chili Beer Baste, continued

4. Remove Chili Beer Baste from refrigerator; reserve 1 cup for table service. Begin basting chicken on grill. Brush chicken generously with Chili Beer Baste sauce during last 10 minutes of cooking. Internal temperature should reach 175°F when tested with meat thermometer inserted near leg joint. Serve chicken with warmed, reserved sauce.

Makes 8 servings

Best Corned Beef Ever

1 to 2 beef briskets (about 5 pounds total)
2 cups apple cider, divided
1 head garlic, cloves separated, crushed and peeled
2 tablespoons whole peppercorns
2 tablespoons dried thyme leaves *or* 1 cup fresh thyme
1 tablespoon mustard seed
1 tablespoon Cajun seasoning
1 teaspoon ground allspice
1 teaspoon ground cumin
1 teaspoon celery seed
2 to 4 cloves
1 bottle (12 ounces) dark beer

Slow Cooker Directions
1. Place brisket, ½ cup cider, garlic, peppercorns, thyme, mustard seed, Cajun seasoning, allspice, cumin, celery seed and cloves in large resealable plastic food storage bag to marinate. Seal and refrigerate overnight.

2. Place brisket and marinade in slow cooker. Add remaining 1½ cups apple cider and beer. Cover; cook on LOW 10 hours. Strain sauce and pour over meat.

Makes 12 servings

Note: Top this tasty beef with Swiss cheese and serve it on a toasted roll.

Mustard-Glazed Ribs

3/4 cup beer
1/2 cup firmly packed dark brown sugar
1/2 cup spicy brown mustard
3 tablespoons soy sauce
1 tablespoon catsup
3/4 teaspoon TABASCO® brand Pepper Sauce
1/2 teaspoon ground cloves
4 pounds pork spareribs or baby back ribs

Combine beer, sugar, mustard, soy sauce, catsup, TABASCO® Sauce and cloves in medium bowl; mix well. Position grill rack as far from coals as possible. Place ribs on grill over low heat. For spareribs, grill 45 minutes; turn occasionally. Brush with mustard glaze. Grill 30 minutes longer or until meat is cooked through; turn and baste often. (For baby back ribs, grill 15 minutes. Brush with mustard glaze. Grill 30 minutes longer or until meat is cooked to desired doneness; turn and baste often.) Heat any remaining glaze to a boil; serve with ribs.

Makes 4 servings

Tip: Make a pungent basting sauce with a rich stout or barleywine.

Bonnie's Slow-Cooked Turkey Thighs With Potatoes

1 large onion, cut into slices
2 turkey thighs, skin removed
2 cloves garlic, minced
1/2 teaspoon black pepper
8 to 10 small red potatoes
1 can (12 ounces) beer
1 can (8 ounces) tomato sauce
1 bay leaf

Slow Cooker Directions
1. Place onion slices in slow cooker. Arrange turkey thighs over onions; sprinkle with garlic and pepper.

2. Place potatoes around turkey thighs. Add beer, tomato sauce and bay leaf. Cover; cook on LOW 8 to 10 hours. Remove and discard bay leaf before serving. *Makes 2 to 4 servings*

Milwaukee Pork Stew

2 pounds boneless pork shoulder or sirloin, cut into $1/2$-inch cubes
$1/3$ cup all-purpose flour
$1\frac{1}{2}$ teaspoons salt
$1/4$ teaspoon black pepper
2 tablespoons vegetable oil
4 large onions, sliced $1/2$ inch thick
1 clove garlic, minced
1 can ($14\frac{1}{2}$ ounces) chicken broth
1 can (12 ounces) beer
$1/4$ cup chopped fresh parsley
2 tablespoons red wine vinegar
1 tablespoon packed brown sugar
1 teaspoon caraway seeds
1 bay leaf

Coat pork with combined flour, salt and pepper. Heat oil in Dutch oven; brown meat over medium-high heat. Add onions and garlic. Cook and stir 5 minutes. Pour off drippings. Stir in remaining ingredients. Bring to a boil. Cover; cook over medium-low heat 1 to $1\frac{1}{4}$ hours or until meat is very tender. Stir occasionally.

Makes 8 servings

Preparation Time: 10 minutes
Cooking Time: 90 minutes

*Favorite recipe from **National Pork Board***

Braised Lamb Shanks with Jarlsberg

Lamb
>   4 lamb shanks (about 1 pound each)
>   2 tablespoons Lucini Premium Select extra virgin olive oil
>   1 chopped onion
>   2 minced garlic cloves
>   1 1/2 cups beer
>   1 1/2 cups beef broth

Coating
>   1 cup (4 ounces) shredded JARLSBERG cheese
>   1 cup flavored bread crumbs
>   1 teaspoon crumbled dried rosemary
>   Freshly ground black pepper, to taste
>   2/3 cup cooking liquid from lamb shanks

In large, heavy skillet, brown 4 shanks in olive oil. Add onion and garlic. Cook until golden. Add beer and beef broth; cover and simmer 1 1/2 hours or until fork tender. Remove to platter. To reduce cooking liquid, cook over high heat 5 minutes. Strain, defat and set aside.

Preheat oven to 325°F. Combine cheese with bread crumbs, rosemary, pepper and cooking liquid. Divide mixture into 4 parts. Pat firmly on meaty tops and sides of lamb shanks to "blanket." Place shanks on rack in baking pan. Bake 15 to 20 minutes or until coating is firm and nearly crisp. Serve with white beans, salad and crusty bread. Serve remaining pan juices in gravy boat.   *Makes 4 servings*

Tip: Braise the lamb in a nutty brown ale to complement the garlic and Jarlsberg cheese.

Braised Lamb Shank with Jarlsberg

BEER *and* CHEESE

Match the Robust Flavors of Cheese With Malt

Zesty Cheese Fondue

1 package (1.8 ounces) white sauce mix
2 cups beer or nonalcoholic malt beverage
1 clove garlic, minced
1 package (16 ounces) pasteurized process cheese spread, cubed
3 tablespoons *Frank's*® *RedHot*® Original Cayenne Pepper
   Sauce
1 loaf French or Italian bread, cubed
   Apple slices

1. Prepare white sauce mix in large saucepan according to package directions except substitute beer for milk and add garlic. Stir in cheese; cook, stirring constantly, until cheese melts and sauce is smooth. Stir in *Frank's RedHot* Sauce.

2. Transfer sauce to fondue pot or heated chafing dish. Serve warm with bread cubes or apple slices.   *Makes 16 servings (4 cups)*

Tip: A dark bock beer will add toasty aromas to complement the bread used for dipping into this fondue.

Prep Time: 15 minutes
Cook Time: 10 minutes

Zesty Cheese Fondue

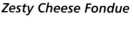

Wisconsin Gorgonzola Ale Sauce

5 pounds onions, diced
¾ cup olive oil
1½ cups amber ale
   Salt and pepper to taste
2 teaspoons dried thyme
   Zest of two lemons, finely chopped
¼ cup minced chives
¼ cup minced red bell pepper
1½ pounds Wisconsin Gorgonzola, crumbled

Caramelize onion in oil over low heat until reduced by half and golden brown. Stir in ale and season with salt, pepper and thyme; cook over low heat until reduced by one third. Stir in lemon zest and reserve.*

To serve, heat onion-beer mixture until it simmers. Add chives and bell pepper; stir well. Cook 1 minute. Remove from heat and stir in crumbled Gorgonzola. Serve immediately over grilled steak or chicken.   *Makes 12 servings*

The onion-ale mixture may be prepared up to 48 hours before serving and held refrigerated in a covered dish.

Favorite recipe from **Wisconsin Milk Marketing Board**

Pilsner Parmesan Potatoes

4 pounds Yukon Gold potatoes, peeled and thinly sliced
1 cup minced Vidalia onion
12 ounces pilsner beer
1 cup grated aged Parmesan cheese
$^1/_2$ cup heavy cream
1 tablespoon flour
1 teaspoon paprika
Salt and pepper to taste

1. Preheat oven to 350°F. Butter 13×9-inch baking dish.

2. Place potato slices in prepared dish. Sprinkle with minced onion.

3. Combine beer, Parmesan cheese, cream, flour, paprika, salt and pepper in medium bowl. Pour over potato-onion mixture; stir gently to coat potato slices evenly. Cover baking dish with foil.

4. Bake 30 minutes. Remove foil; bake 15 to 20 minutes or until potatoes are golden brown and bubbly.

5. Remove from oven; let stand 15 minutes before serving.

Makes 4 to 6 servings

Bacon and Cheese Rarebit

12 slices bacon
1 small loaf (8 ounces) egg bread or challah, cut into
    6 (1-inch-thick) slices
1½ tablespoons butter or margarine
½ cup amber or Vienna lager beer
2 teaspoons Worcestershire sauce
2 teaspoons Dijon mustard
⅛ teaspoon ground red pepper
1 cup (4 ounces) shredded brick cheese
2 cups (8 ounces) shredded sharp Cheddar cheese
12 large slices ripe tomato

1. Cook bacon in large skillet over medium-high heat about 7 minutes or until crisp. Remove bacon to paper towels.

2. Toast bread slices until golden brown. Cover and keep warm.

3. Preheat broiler. Meanwhile, melt butter in double boiler set over simmering water. Stir in beer, Worcestershire, mustard and red pepper; heat through.

4. Add cheeses, stirring constantly about 1 minute or until cheeses are melted. Remove from heat; cover and keep warm.

5. Arrange toast on greased or foil-lined 15×10-inch jelly-roll pan. Top each serving with 2 tomato slices and 2 strips bacon. Spoon about ¼ cup cheese sauce evenly over each serving. Broil 4 to 5 inches from heat 2 to 3 minutes or until cheese begins to brown. Transfer to individual serving plates. Garnish with fresh herbs, if desired. Serve immediately.   *Makes 6 servings*

Bacon and Cheese Rarebit

Ale Cheese-Stuffed Pattypans

4 pattypan squash (about 3 inches in diameter)
4 tablespoons butter or margarine
2 ribs celery, diced
$^1/_2$ cup chopped onion
$^1/_2$ cup amber ale
1 cup dry herb-seasoned stuffing mix
1 cup shredded sharp Cheddar cheese

1. Preheat oven to 350°F. To prepare pattypans, wash and slice off top, above scalloped edge; discard tops. Scoop out seeds and discard.

2. Place squash shells in large skillet. Pour $^1/_4$ inch of water into skillet; cover. Bring to a boil over high heat. Reduce heat to medium-low; simmer 5 minutes. Transfer squash, cut side up, to greased 8×8-inch baking dish.

3. Heat butter in large skillet over medium-high heat until melted and bubbly. Cook and stir celery and onion in hot butter until tender. Add ale, then stuffing mix. Stir to absorb liquid. Stir in cheese. Divide mixture among squash.

4. Bake 20 to 30 minutes or until squash is fork-tender and stuffing is lightly browned. Garnish as desired. Serve immediately.

Makes 4 side-dish servings

Ale Cheese-Stuffed Pattypans

Cheddar and Leek Strata

8 eggs, lightly beaten
2 cups milk
$^1/_2$ cup porter ale
2 cloves garlic, minced
$^1/_4$ teaspoon salt
$^1/_4$ teaspoon black pepper
1 loaf (16 ounces) sourdough bread, cut into $^1/_2$-inch cubes
2 small leeks, coarsely chopped
1 red bell pepper, chopped
1$^1/_2$ cups (6 ounces) shredded Swiss cheese
1$^1/_2$ cups (6 ounces) shredded sharp Cheddar cheese
Fresh sage sprigs, for garnish

1. Combine eggs, milk, ale, garlic, salt and black pepper in large bowl. Beat until well blended.

2. Place $^1/_2$ of bread cubes on bottom of greased 13×9-inch baking dish. Sprinkle half of leeks and half of bell pepper over bread cubes. Top with $^3/_4$ cup Swiss cheese and $^3/_4$ cup Cheddar cheese. Repeat layers with remaining ingredients, ending with Cheddar cheese.

3. Pour egg mixture evenly over top. Cover tightly with plastic wrap or foil. Weigh top of strata down with slightly smaller baking dish. Refrigerate strata at least 2 hours or overnight.

4. Preheat oven to 350°F. Bake, uncovered, 40 to 45 minutes or until center is set. Garnish with fresh sage, if desired. Serve immediately.

Makes 12 servings

Cheddar and Leek Strata

Beer Cheese Dip

2 cups shredded Cheddar cheese
2 packages (8 ounces each) cream cheese, softened
1 packet (1 ounce) HIDDEN VALLEY® The Original Ranch®
    Salad Dressing & Seasoning Mix
$^1/_2$ to $^3/_4$ cup beer
    Chopped green onion and additional Cheddar cheese

In medium bowl, combine Cheddar cheese, cream cheese and salad dressing & seasoning mix. Gradually stir in beer until mixture is to desired consistency. Garnish with green onion and additional Cheddar cheese. Serve with pretzels or assorted fresh vegetables, if desired.   *Makes about 3 cups*

Tip: An American amber ale, with strong hops character, works well in this recipe.

Wisconsin Gouda and Beer Spread

2 pounds Wisconsin Gouda Cheese*
$^3/_4$ cup butter, cubed and softened
2 tablespoons snipped fresh chives
2 teaspoons Dijon mustard
$^1/_2$ cup amber ale, at room temperature
    Cocktail rye or pumpernickel bread slices

*Cut $^1/_5$ from top of cheese to create flat surface. With butter curler or melon baller, remove cheese from center of ball, leaving $^1/_2$-inch-thick shell. Shred enough of cheese removed from ball and top to measure 4 cups. Reserve remaining cheese for another use.

In large bowl, place shredded cheese, butter, chives and mustard; mix with spoon until blended. Stir in beer until blended. Spoon spread into hollowed cheese ball; reserve remaining spread for refills. Chill until serving time. Serve with cocktail bread.   *Makes 4 cups*

Favorite recipe from **Wisconsin Milk Marketing Board**

Beer Cheese Dip

HOPS TO IT!

Just a Dash of Beer for Easy Dinners

Patrick's Irish Lamb Soup

1 tablespoon olive oil
1 medium onion, coarsely chopped
1½ pounds fresh lean American lamb boneless shoulder, cut
  into ¾-inch cubes
1 bottle (12 ounces) beer *or* ¾ cup water
1 teaspoon seasoned pepper
2 cans (14½ ounces each) beef broth
1 package (0.93 ounces) brown gravy mix
3 cups cubed potatoes
2 cups thinly sliced carrots
2 cups shredded green cabbage
⅓ cup chopped fresh parsley (optional)

In 3-quart saucepan with cover, heat oil. Add onion and sauté until brown, stirring occasionally. Add lamb and sauté, stirring until browned. Stir in beer and pepper. Cover and simmer 30 minutes. Mix in broth and gravy mix. Add potatoes and carrots; cover and simmer 15 to 20 minutes or until vegetables are tender. Stir in cabbage and cook just until cabbage turns bright green. Garnish with chopped parsley, if desired.   *Makes 8 servings*

*Favorite recipe from **American Lamb Council***

Patrick's Irish Lamb Soup

Fish & Chips

¾ cup all-purpose flour
½ cup India pale ale
   Vegetable oil
4 medium russet potatoes, each cut into 8 wedges
   Salt
1 egg, separated
1 pound cod fillets (about 6 to 8 small fillets)
   Malt vinegar (optional)

1. Combine flour, ale and 2 teaspoons oil in small bowl. Cover; refrigerate 1 to 2 hours.

2. Pour 2 inches of oil into heavy skillet. Heat over medium heat until fresh bread cube placed in oil browns in 45 seconds (about 365°F). Add potato wedges. (Do not crowd.) Fry potato wedges 4 to 6 minutes or until outsides are brown, turning once. Drain on paper towels; sprinkle lightly with salt. Repeat with remaining potato wedges. (Allow temperature of oil to return to 365°F between batches.) Reserve oil to fry cod.

3. Stir egg yolk into reserved flour mixture. Beat egg white with electric mixer at high speed in medium bowl until soft peaks form. Fold egg white into flour mixture; set aside.

4. Rinse fish; pat dry with paper towels. Cut fish into 8 pieces. Dip 4 fish pieces into batter; fry 4 to 6 minutes or until batter is crispy and brown and fish flakes easily when tested with fork, turning once. Drain on paper towels. Repeat with remaining fish pieces. (Allow temperature of oil to return to 365°F between batches.) Serve immediately with potato wedges. Sprinkle with malt vinegar and garnish, if desired.   *Makes 4 servings*

Fajitas With Amber Lager

1 beef flank steak (1¼ to 1½ pounds)

12 ounces Mexican amber lager

3 tablespoons fresh lime juice

1 tablespoon seeded and minced jalapeño pepper*

2 large cloves garlic, minced

Avocado Salsa (page 72)

8 (6- or 7-inch) flour tortillas

1 large red bell pepper, cut lengthwise into 4 strips

1 large green bell pepper, cut lengthwise into 4 strips

4 slices red onion, cut ¼ inch thick

*Jalapeño peppers can sting and irritate the skin; wear rubber gloves when handling peppers and do not touch eyes. Wash hands after handling peppers.

1. Place steak in large resealable plastic food storage bag. Combine lager, lime juice, jalapeño and garlic in small bowl; pour over steak. Seal bag tightly, turning to coat. Marinate in refrigerator 1 to 4 hours, turning once.

2. Prepare grill for direct cooking.

3. Meanwhile, prepare Avocado Salsa. Wrap tortillas in heavy-duty foil.

4. Drain steak; discard marinade. Place steak, bell peppers and onion slices on grid over medium heat. Grill, uncovered, 17 to 21 minutes for medium rare to medium or until desired doneness. Turn steak, bell peppers and onion slices halfway through grilling time. Place tortilla packet on grid during last 5 to 7 minutes of grilling; turn halfway through grilling time to heat through.

5. Transfer steak to carving board. Carve steak across the grain into thin slices. Slice bell peppers into thin strips. Separate onion slices into rings. Divide among tortillas; roll up and top with Avocado Salsa.

Makes 4 servings

continued on page 72

Fajitas With Amber Lager

Fajitas with Amber Lager, continued

Avocado Salsa

1 large ripe avocado, coarsely chopped
1 large tomato, seeded and diced
3 tablespoons chopped fresh cilantro
1 tablespoon vegetable oil
1 tablespoon fresh lime juice
2 teaspoons minced fresh or drained, bottled jalapeño pepper*
1 clove garlic, minced
$^{1}/_{2}$ teaspoon salt

Jalapeño peppers can sting and irritate the skin; wear rubber gloves when handling peppers and do not touch eyes. Wash hands after handling peppers.

1. Place avocado in medium bowl.

2. Gently stir in tomato, cilantro, oil, lime juice, jalapeño, garlic and salt until well combined. Let stand at room temperature while grilling steak. Cover and refrigerate if preparing in advance. Bring to room temperature before serving.   *Makes about 1$^{1}/_{2}$ cups*

Polska Kielbasa Simmered in Beer and Onions

4 tablespoons butter
4 onions, thinly sliced
1 pound HILLSHIRE FARM® Polska Kielbasa, diagonally
     sliced into $^{1}/_{4}$-inch pieces
1 bottle (12 ounces) beer

Melt butter in large skillet over medium heat; sauté onions 4 to 5 minutes. Add Polska Kielbasa; brown 3 to 4 minutes on each side. Pour beer into skillet; bring to a boil. Reduce heat and simmer, uncovered, 25 minutes.   *Makes 4 to 6 servings*

Chicken Vera Cruz

1 chicken (3 pounds), cut up
1 jar (12 ounces) salsa
1⅓ cups *French's*® French Fried Onions, divided
½ cup Spanish stuffed olives, sliced
½ cup beer or nonalcoholic malt beverage
2 tablespoons lemon juice
2 tablespoons chopped fresh parsley *or* 1 tablespoon dried
    parsley leaves
¼ teaspoon ground black pepper
Cooked white rice (optional)

Preheat oven to 350°F. Place chicken in 2-quart shallow dish. Bake, uncovered, 40 minutes. Drain.

Combine salsa, ⅔ *cup* French Fried Onions, olives, beer, lemon juice, parsley and pepper in medium saucepan. Bring to a boil. Reduce heat to low. Cook and stir 5 minutes or until slightly thickened. Pour sauce over chicken. Bake 15 minutes or until chicken is no longer pink near bone. Sprinkle with remaining ⅔ *cup* onions. Bake 5 minutes or until onions are golden. Serve with rice, if desired.   *Makes 4 to 6 servings*

Prep Time: 15 minutes
Cook Time: 60 minutes

Tip: For authentic flavor, try adding a Mexican light lager to this variation on arroz con pollo.

Ale-Steamed Crabs
With Corn on the Cob

2 bottles (24 ounces) amber ale
1 pint cider vinegar or white vinegar
2 dozen live small crabs
½ pound seafood seasoning
½ pound salt
4 ears fresh corn, cooked

1. Place ale and vinegar in 10-gallon stockpot. Place rack in bottom of pot. Place half of crabs on rack. Mix seafood seasoning with salt; sprinkle half over crabs.

2. Repeat layering with remaining crabs and seasoning mixture.

3. Cover pot. Cook over high heat until liquid begins to steam. Steam about 25 minutes or until crabs turn red and meat is white. Remove crabs to large serving platter, using tongs.

4. Cover table with disposable paper cloth.

5. To pick crabs, place crab on its back. With thumb or knife point, pry off "apron" flap (the "pull tab"-looking shell in the center) and discard.

6. Lift off top shell and discard.

7. Break off toothed claws and set aside. With knife edge, scrape off 3 areas of lungs and debris over hard semi-transparent membrane covering edible crabmeat.

8. Hold crab at each side; break apart at center. Discard legs. Remove membrane cover with knife, exposing large chunks of meat; remove with fingers or knife.

9. Crack claws with mallet or knife handle to expose meat.

10. Serve with corn on the cob. *Makes 4 servings*

Ale-Steamed Crabs
With Corn on the Cob

Hickory Beef Kabobs

1 pound boneless beef top sirloin or tenderloin steaks, cut
     into $1^{1}/_{4}$-inch pieces
2 ears fresh corn,* shucked, cleaned and cut crosswise into
     1-inch pieces
1 red or green bell pepper, cut into 1-inch squares
1 small red onion, cut into $^{1}/_{2}$-inch wedges
$^{1}/_{2}$ cup stout
$^{1}/_{2}$ cup chili sauce
1 teaspoon dry mustard
2 cloves garlic, minced
3 cups hot cooked white rice
$^{1}/_{4}$ cup chopped fresh parsley

Four small ears frozen corn, thawed, can be substituted for fresh corn.

1. Place beef, corn, bell pepper and onion in large resealable plastic food storage bag. Combine stout, chili sauce, mustard and garlic in small bowl; pour over beef and vegetables. Seal bag tightly, turning to coat. Marinate in refrigerator at least 1 hour or up to 8 hours, turning occasionally.

2. Prepare grill for direct cooking. Meanwhile, cover $1^{1}/_{2}$ cups hickory chips with cold water; soak 20 minutes.

3. Drain beef and vegetables; reserve marinade. Alternately thread beef and vegetables onto 4 (12-inch) metal skewers. Brush with reserved marinade.

4. Drain hickory chips; sprinkle over coals. Place kabobs on grid. Grill kabobs, uncovered, over medium heat 5 minutes. Brush with reserved marinade; turn and brush again. Discard remaining marinade. Continue to grill 5 to 7 minutes for medium or until desired doneness.

5. Combine rice and chopped parsley; serve kabobs over rice mixture.

Makes 4 servings

Hickory Beef Kabob

Brewed Beef Enchiladas

1 sheet (20×12 inches) heavy-duty foil, generously sprayed
    with nonstick cooking spray
6 ounces 95% lean ground beef
1/4 cup sliced green onions
1 teaspoon fresh minced or bottled garlic
1 cup (4 ounces) shredded Mexican cheese blend or Cheddar
    cheese, divided
3/4 cup chopped tomato, divided
1/2 cup frozen corn, thawed
1/3 cup cold cooked white or brown rice
1/4 cup salsa or picante sauce
6 (6- to 7-inch) corn tortillas
1/2 cup Mexican lager
1/2 cup mild or hot red or green enchilada sauce
1/2 cup sliced romaine lettuce leaves

1. Preheat oven to 375°F. Place foil in 9×9-inch or 8×8-inch square baking pan.

2. Cook ground beef in medium nonstick skillet over medium heat until no longer pink; drain. Add green onions and garlic; cook and stir 2 minutes.

3. Combine meat mixture, 3/4 cup cheese, 1/2 cup tomato, corn, rice and salsa; mix well. Spoon mixture down center of tortillas. Roll up; place, seam side down, in prepared pan. Combine lager and enchilada sauce in small bowl; spoon evenly over enchiladas.

4. Double fold sides and ends of foil to seal packets, leaving head space for heat circulation. Place packets on baking sheet.

5. Bake 15 minutes or until hot. Remove from oven. Sprinkle with remaining 1/4 cup cheese; bake 10 minutes more. Transfer contents to serving plates; serve with lettuce and remaining 1/4 cup tomato.

Makes 2 servings

Prep Time: 15 minutes
Cook Time: 35 minutes

SIDES with SUDS

Fresh Vegetables and Side Dishes Made Malty

Boston Baked Beans

3 cans (15 or 16 ounces each) navy or Great Northern beans,
    rinsed and drained
1 bottle (12 ounces) India pale ale
1 cup minced sweet onion
$^1/_3$ cup ketchup
$^1/_3$ cup maple syrup
2 teaspoons Worcestershire sauce
1 teaspoon dry mustard
$^1/_2$ teaspoon ground ginger
4 slices bacon

1. Preheat oven to 350°F. Place beans in 11×7-inch glass baking dish. Combine ale, onion, ketchup, maple syrup, Worcestershire sauce, mustard and ginger in medium bowl. Pour over beans; toss to coat.

2. Cut bacon into 1-inch pieces; arrange in single layer over beans. Bake, uncovered, 40 to 45 minutes or until most of liquid is absorbed and bacon is browned.

Makes 8 servings

Boston Baked Beans

Polenta Triangles With Amber Ale

$^1\!/_2$ cup yellow corn grits
$^1\!/_2$ cup amber ale
  1 cup chicken broth, divided
  2 cloves garlic, minced
$^1\!/_2$ cup (2 ounces) crumbled feta cheese
  1 red bell pepper, roasted,* peeled and finely chopped
    Nonstick cooking spray

Place pepper on foil-lined broiler pan; broil 15 minutes or until blackened on all sides, turning every 5 minutes. Place pepper in paper bag; close bag and let stand 15 minutes before peeling.

1. Combine grits and ale; mix well. Set aside.

2. Pour chicken broth into large heavy saucepan; bring to a boil. Add garlic and moistened grits; mix well and return to a boil. Reduce heat to low; cover and cook 20 minutes. Remove from heat; add feta cheese. Stir until cheese is completely melted. Add bell pepper; mix well.

3. Spray 8-inch square baking pan with cooking spray. Spoon grits mixture into prepared pan. Press grits evenly into pan. Refrigerate until cold.

4. Preheat broiler. Turn polenta out onto cutting board; cut into 2-inch squares. Cut each square diagonally into 2 triangles.

5. Spray baking sheet with cooking spray. Place polenta triangles on prepared baking sheet and spray tops lightly with cooking spray. Place under broiler until lightly browned. Turn triangles over and broil until browned and crisp. Serve warm or at room temperature. Garnish with fresh oregano and chives, if desired.   *Makes 6 to 8 servings*

Polenta Triangles With Amber Ale

The Ultimate Onion

3 cups cornstarch
3½ cups all-purpose flour, divided
6 teaspoons paprika, divided
2 teaspoons garlic salt
1 teaspoon salt
1½ teaspoons black pepper, divided
2 bottles (24 ounces) beer
4 to 6 Colossal onions (4 inches in diameter)
2 teaspoons garlic powder
¾ teaspoon cayenne pepper, divided
1 pint (2 cups) *each* mayonnaise and sour cream
½ cup chili sauce

1. For batter, mix cornstarch, 1½ cups flour, 2 teaspoons paprika, garlic salt, salt and 1 teaspoon black pepper in large bowl. Add beer; mix well. Set aside.

2. Cut about ¾ inch off top of each onion. Peel onions. Being careful not to cut through bottom, cut each onion into 12 to 16 wedges. Soak in ice water 10 to 15 minutes. If onions do not "bloom," cut petals slightly deeper. Meanwhile, prepare seasoned flour mixture. Combine remaining 2 cups flour, remaining 4 teaspoons paprika, garlic powder, remaining ½ teaspoon black pepper and ¼ teaspoon cayenne pepper in large bowl; mix well.

3. Dip onions into seasoned flour; remove excess by carefully shaking. Dip in batter; remove excess. Separate "petals" to coat thoroughly with batter. (If batter begins to separate, mix thoroughly before using.) Gently place onions, one at a time, in fryer basket and deep-fry at 375°F 1½ minutes. Turn onion over and fry 1 to 1½ minutes or until golden brown. Drain on paper towels. Place onion upright in shallow bowl and remove about 1 inch of "petals" from center.

4. To prepare Creamy Chili Sauce, combine mayonnaise, sour cream, chili sauce and remaining ½ teaspoon cayenne pepper in large bowl; mix well. Serve with warm onions. *Makes about 24 servings*

*Favorite recipe from **National Onion Association***

Beer Batter Tempura

1 1/2 cups all purpose flour
1 1/2 cups Asian lager, well chilled
1 teaspoon salt
Dipping Sauce (recipe follows)
Vegetable oil for frying
1/2 pound green beans or asparagus tips
1 large sweet potato, peeled and cut into 1/4-inch slices
1 medium eggplant, cut into 1/4-inch slices

1. Combine flour, lager and salt in medium bowl just until mixed; set aside 15 minutes. Batter should be thin and lumpy. (Do not overmix.) Meanwhile, prepare Dipping Sauce.

2. Heat 1 inch of oil in saucepan to 375°F. Maintain temperature throughout cooking.

3. Dip 5 to 6 green beans in batter; add to hot oil. Fry until light golden brown. Remove to wire racks or paper towels to drain. Repeat with remaining vegetables. Fry vegetable types separately. Serve with Dipping Sauce. *Makes 4 servings*

Dipping Sauce

1/2 cup soy sauce
2 tablespoons rice wine
1 tablespoon sugar
1/2 teaspoon white vinegar
2 teaspoons minced fresh ginger
1 teaspoon minced fresh garlic
2 scallions, thinly sliced

Combine soy sauce, rice wine, sugar and vinegar in small saucepan over medium heat. Cook and stir 3 minutes or until sugar dissolves. Add ginger and garlic; cook 2 minutes. Add scallions; remove from heat.
Make 4 servings

Malty Maple Corn Bread

1 cup coarse ground cornmeal
1 cup porter or dark ale
$\frac{1}{4}$ cup maple syrup
1 cup all-purpose flour
$\frac{1}{2}$ teaspoon salt
1 tablespoon baking powder
2 large eggs
$\frac{1}{4}$ cup melted butter

1. Preheat oven to 400°F. Combine cornmeal, porter and maple syrup in small bowl; set aside.

2. Sift flour, salt and baking powder into large bowl. Add cornmeal mixture, eggs and melted butter. Stir until well blended.

3. Pour batter into greased 9-inch square pan. Bake until wooden pick inserted into center comes out clean, about 20 to 25 minutes. Cool 10 minutes. Slice and serve.   *Makes 8 servings*

Note: For an extra-flavorful crust, place the greased pan in the oven for several minutes to preheat. When batter is ready, pour into hot pan and bake as directed. The corn bread will develop a thick, brown crust with a deep, rich flavor.

Asparagus with Honey-Garlic Sauce

1 pound asparagus
$^1/_4$ cup Dijon mustard
$^1/_4$ cup dark ale or beer
3 tablespoons honey
$^1/_2$ teaspoon minced garlic
$^1/_4$ teaspoon crushed dried thyme leaves
$^1/_4$ teaspoon salt

Add asparagus to boiling, salted water; cook, covered, about 2 minutes or until barely tender. Drain. Combine mustard, ale, honey, garlic, thyme and salt; mix well. Pour over asparagus.   *Makes 4 servings*

Tip: A porter ale works well in this recipe.

Favorite recipe from **National Honey Board**

Lickety-Split Beer Rolls

PAM® No-Stick Cooking Spray
4 cups self-rising flour
$^1/_4$ cup sugar
1 teaspoon salt
2 cups beer
$^1/_2$ cup WESSON® Canola Oil
1 $^1/_2$ tablespoons caraway seeds

Preheat oven to 400°F. Spray muffin cups with PAM® Cooking Spray. In large mixing bowl, combine flour, sugar and salt; blend well. Add beer and Wesson® Oil; stir until dry ingredients are moistened. Fold in caraway seeds. Fill muffin cups to rim with batter; bake 30 to 35 minutes or until tops are golden brown. Cool for 5 minutes. Remove rolls from pan; cool on wire rack. Serve warm or cool.
Makes 1 $^1/_2$ dozen rolls

Asparagus with Honey-Garlic Sauce

German Rye Beer Bread

1½-Pound Loaf
  1¼ cups beer, at room temperature
    2 tablespoons light molasses
    1 tablespoon butter
1½ teaspoons salt
    2 teaspoons caraway seeds
2½ cups bread flour
  ½ cup rye flour
1½ teaspoons rapid-rise yeast

2-Pound Loaf
  1½ cups beer, at room temperature
    3 tablespoons light molasses
1½ tablespoons butter
    2 teaspoons salt
    1 tablespoon caraway seeds
3¼ cups bread flour
  ¾ cup rye flour
    2 teaspoons rapid-rise yeast

Bread Machine Method
1. Measuring carefully, place all ingredients in bread machine pan in order specified by owner's manual.

2. Program basic cycle and desired crust setting; press start. Remove baked bread from pan; cool on wire rack.   *Makes 12 or 16 servings*

German Rye Beer Bread

Acknowledgments

The publisher would like to thank the companies and organizations listed below for the use of their recipes and photographs in this publication.

American Lamb Council

ConAgra Foods®

The Hidden Valley® Food Products Company

Hillshire Farm®

Hormel Foods, LLC

The Kingsford Products Company

McIlhenny Company (TABASCO® brand Pepper Sauce)

National Honey Board

National Onion Association

National Pork Board

Norseland, Inc. / Lucini Italia Co.

Reckitt Benckiser Inc.

Wisconsin Milk Marketing Board

Index

A
Ale Cheese-Stuffed Pattypans, 60
Ale'd Pork and Sauerkraut, 44
Ale-Steamed Crabs With Corn on the Cob, 74
Asparagus with Honey-Garlic Sauce, 88
Avocado Salsa, 72

B
Bacon (*see also* **Turkey Bacon**): Bacon and
    Cheese Rarebit, 58
Beans
    Bock Bean Bites, 32
    Boston Baked Beans, 80
    Durango Chili, 14
    Hearty Beefy Beer Soup, 8
Beef (*see also* **Beef, Ground**)
    Beef Stock, 10
    Best Corned Beef Ever, 48
    Borracho Beef, 26
    Deviled Beef Short Rib Stew, 18
    Durango Chili, 14
    Fajitas With Amber Lager, 70
    Hearty Beefy Beer Soup, 8
    Hickory Beef Kabobs, 76
    Spicy Italian Beef, 42
Beef, Ground
    Brewed Beef Enchiladas, 78
    Dark Ale and Dill Burgers, 31
    Durango Chili, 14
    Stout Beef Bundles, 38
Beef Stock, 10
Beer Batter Tempura, 86
Beer Cheese Dip, 64
Best Corned Beef Ever, 48
Bock Bean Bites, 32
Bonnie's Slow-Cooked Turkey Thighs With
    Potatoes, 50
Borracho Beef, 26
Boston Baked Beans, 80
Braised Lamb Shanks with Jarlsberg, 52
Brats 'n' Beer, 34
Brats in Beer, 24
Bread
    Bacon and Cheese Rarebit, 58
    Cheddar and Leek Strata, 6
    German Rye Beer Bread, 90
    Malty Maple Corn Bread, 87
    Zesty Cheese Fondue, 54
Brewed Beef Enchiladas, 78
Burgers: Dark Ale and Dill Burgers, 31

C
Cabbage
    Kielbasa & Cabbage Soup, 16
    Patrick's Irish Lamb Soup, 66
Cajun Chicken Nuggets & Grilled Fruit, 30
Cheddar and Leek Strata, 62
Cheese, 54–65
    Bock Bean Bites, 32
    Brewed Beef Enchiladas, 78
    Durango Chili, 14

Farmer's Market Grilled Chowder,
    12
Ham and Beer Cheese Soup, 17
Milwaukee Pork Stew, 52
Polenta Triangles With Amber Ale, 82
Wisconsin Cheddar, Swiss and Beer Soup,
    11
Wisconsin Edam and Beer Spread, 37
Wisconsin Sausage Soup, 20
Chicken
    Cajun Chicken Nuggets & Grilled Fruit,
        30
    Chicken Vera Cruz, 73
    Chicken Wings in Cerveza, 40
    Grilled Chicken With Chili Beer Baste,
        46
Chicken Vera Cruz, 73
Chicken Wings in Cerveza, 40
Corn
    Ale-Steamed Crabs With Corn on the Cob,
        74
    Brewed Beef Enchiladas, 78
    Farmer's Market Grilled Chowder, 12
    Hickory Beef Kabobs, 76
    Polenta Triangles With Amber Ale, 82
Corn Bread: Malty Maple Corn Bread,
    87
Creamy Chili Sauce, 84

D
Dark Ale and Dill Burgers, 31
Deviled Beef Short Rib Stew, 18
Dipping Sauce, 28, 86
Dips & Sauces
    Avocado Salsa, 72
    Beer Cheese Dip, 64
    Creamy Chili Sauce, 84
    Dipping Sauce, 28, 86
    Wisconsin Gorgonzola Ale Sauce, 56
    Zesty Cheese Fondue, 54
Durango Chili, 14

E
Eggplant: Beer Batter Tempura, 86
Enchiladas: Brewed Beef Enchiladas, 78

F
Fajitas With Amber Lager, 70
Farmer's Market Grilled Chowder, 12
Fish: Fish & Chips, 68

G
German Rye Beer Bread, 90
Glaze: Peachy Mustard Glaze, 30
Grilled Chicken With Chili Beer Baste,
    46

H
Ham: Ham and Beer Cheese Soup, 17
Hearty Beefy Beer Soup, 8
Hickory Beef Kabobs, 76

K

Kabobs: Hickory Beef Kabobs, 76
Kielbasa & Cabbage Soup, 16
Kielbasa & Kraut Heroes, 36

L

Lamb
    Braised Lamb Shanks with Jarlsberg, 52
    Patrick's Irish Lamb Soup, 66
    Porter Portobello Mushrooms, 31
    Western Lamb Riblets, 36
Lettuce
    Brewed Beef Enchiladas, 78
    Stout Beef Bundles, 38
Lickety-Split Beer Rolls, 88

M

Malty Maple Corn Bread, 87
Milwaukee Pork Stew, 51
Mushrooms
    Hearty Beefy Beer Soup, 8
    Porter Portobello Mushrooms, 31
Mussels in Beer Broth Over Pasta, 22
Mustard-Glazed Ribs, 50

O

Onions, Colossal: The Ultimate Onion, 84

P

Pasta: Mussels in Beer Broth Over Pasta, 22
Patrick's Irish Lamb Soup, 66
Peachy Mustard Glaze, 30
Pineapple: Cajun Chicken Nuggets & Grilled Fruit, 30
Polenta Triangles With Amber Ale, 82
Polska Kielbasa Simmered in Beer and Onions, 72
Pork (*see also* **Bacon; Ham; Sausage**)
    Ale'd Pork and Sauerkraut, 44
    Milwaukee Pork Stew, 51
    Mustard-Glazed Ribs, 50
Porter Portobello Mushrooms, 31
Potato
    Bonnie's Slow-Cooked Turkey Thighs With Potatoes, 50
    Deviled Beef Short Rib Stew, 18
    Farmer's Market Grilled Chowder, 12
    Fish & Chips, 68
    Patrick's Irish Lamb Soup, 66
    Pilsner Parmesan Potatoes, 57
Potato, Sweet: Beer Batter Tempura, 86

R

Ribs
    Mustard-Glazed Ribs, 50
    Western Lamb Riblets, 36
Rolls: Lickety-Split Beer Rolls, 88

S

Salsa
    Bock Bean Bites, 32
    Chicken Vera Cruz, 73
    Fajitas With Amber Lager, 70
Sauerkraut
    Ale'd Pork and Sauerkraut, 44
    Kielbasa & Kraut Heroes, 36
Sausage
    Brats 'n' Beer, 34
    Brats in Beer, 24
    Kielbasa & Cabbage Soup, 16
    Kielbasa & Kraut Heroes, 36
    Polska Kielbasa Simmered in Beer and Onions, 72
    Wisconsin Sausage Soup, 20
Shellfish
    Ale-Steamed Crabs With Corn on the Cob, 74
    Mussels in Beer Broth Over Pasta, 22
    Spicy Ale Shrimp, 28
Soups & Stews, 8–23
    Milwaukee Pork Stew, 51
    Patrick's Irish Lamb Soup, 66
Spicy Ale Shrimp, 28
Spicy Italian Beef, 42
Spreads
    Wisconsin Edam and Beer Spread, 37
    Wisconsin Gouda and Beer Spread, 64
Squash (*see also* **Zucchini**): Ale Cheese-Stuffed Pattypans, 60
Stock
    Beef Stock, 10
    Hearty Beefy Beer Soup, 8
Stout Beef Bundles, 38
Strata: Cheddar and Leek Strata, 62

T

The Ultimate Onion, 84
Tortillas
    Bock Bean Bites, 32
    Borracho Beef, 26
    Brewed Beef Enchiladas, 78
    Fajitas With Amber Lager, 70
Turkey (*see also* **Turkey Bacon**): Bonnie's Slow-Cooked Turkey Thighs With Potatoes, 50
Turkey Bacon: Boston Baked Beans, 80

W

Western Lamb Riblets, 36
Wisconsin Cheddar, Swiss and Beer Soup, 11
Wisconsin Edam and Beer Spread, 37
Wisconsin Gorgonzola Ale Sauce, 56
Wisconsin Gouda and Beer Spread, 64
Wisconsin Sausage Soup, 20

Z

Zesty Cheese Fondue, 54
Zucchini
    Dark Ale and Dill Burgers, 31
    Farmer's Market Grilled Chowder, 12
    Hearty Beefy Beer Soup, 8